The Book Inside of You

'The Step by Step Guide to Writing, Publishing and Marketing Your Book'

By Fiona Lynch

I0461770

ISBN 978-0-244-36845-6

Acknowledgements

I would first like to thank my Lord Jesus for always giving me the grace to do great things through Him. Secondly, I would like to thank my six children for always supporting me in everything that I do. Thirdly, I would like to thank Joanne James, who has read my work several times and thank you to Sasha Remling for giving her feedback. Your assistance has been much appreciated.

Contents

4

Foreword

Fiona is a published author of five publications, Pastor, teacher, course provider, conference and retreat organiser and public speaker. She is also the Pastor and pioneer of The Church of United Nations in Cambridge, UK and runs The School of DESTINY 'Recreating Lives for a Brighter Future' which consists of courses to rebuild the lives of those that have broken down. She has been on the TV and has appeared in various evangelical newspapers and magazines. She has taught about book writing, publication and marketing on several occasions at the Cambridge Christian Writers Group and as a speaker at one of their annual conferences and hosts several workshops throughout the year teaching her students on how to self-publish their books at a minimal cost. She also teaches this course through her online school, The School of Destiny. I have known Fiona for several years now and have found her to be thorough in all that she does. I am thankful that I know her as I know that she prides herself in all that she does.

By Apostle Michael Blair – Meadowbanks Empowerment Centre, Guyana

This is what some of her students have to say:

"I really enjoyed the book writing course. I gained an invaluable amount of knowledge and improved my skills. I got so much information in much a short space time.

It was unbelievable. I would like to express my gratitude to Pastor Fiona Lynch for giving me the opportunity to increase my learning and understanding."

By Alison Callaghan who attended the one day
The Book Inside of You course

"Before I did this course, I did not know how or where I was going to start my book and now, I have the tools and plans I need to get started. This course was so easy to follow and understand and I would recommend this course to anyone who wants to write a book. The amount of help that is available from Fiona if you have any questions is amazing."

By Joanne James who completed the online course.

Introduction

This guide is written with simplicity and if the teaching is applied you will have the foundation to become successful.

The guide is divided into three parts with questions to answer and actions throughout to assist you with the process of writing, publishing and marketing your book. If you follow the instructions in this guide, you will at least have the draft and foundation of your product. Write your answers to the questions in the spaces where applicable. Where there is referencing to "your manuscript" and/or "your book" this can be applied to any other products that you are publishing.

The first part is Session 1
Preparing Your Manuscript

In this session you will learn how to prepare your manuscript according to who your target audience is. We will focus on three key points 1. the vision, 2. the aim and 3. your audience. All three points are necessary in order to prepare your manuscript.

The second part is Session 2
From Manuscript to Publication

In this session you will learn about putting your manuscript together for it to be published i.e. editing, formatting, the different types of publishing, copyrighting and ISBN numbers.

The third part is Session 3
From Publication to Marketing

Now that your book is published it is that time when there is great joy, but then reality sets in and the question arises, "how do I promote and sell my book?" In this session you will be given the different marketing tools to ensure that you make sales locally within the first three months of publishing your book and promoting international sales.

Preparing Your Manuscript

What is a Manuscript?

A manuscript is either 'a book, document, or piece of music written by hand rather than typed or printed or an author's handwritten or typed text that has not yet been published.' (online dictionary).

A manuscript is therefore a document that is prepared and is ready for publication. It can be a fiction or non-fiction book, a magazine or even a course. With any document it takes time to prepare.

There are three points to consider when preparing your manuscript:

1. The Vision

2. Your Aim

3. Who is your Audience and why are they your Audience?

These three points will set the foundation for the creation of your work.

As a Christian, I had just finished watching the God channel. A well-known preacher had just produced her new book, when I asked the Lord "what next? (what did He want me to do)" It was the school summer holidays and I did not know what to do with my time. I had been in Christ about a year and with six small children, I could not do much. Whilst sitting on my sofa a vision of a book appeared to me. On the cover was the title 'From Darkness to Light' with my name on! I could see the image of the cover as clear as day and I knew there and then that the Lord wanted me to write a book. This book was to be a true story, my story... "But I don't have a computer." I spoke to myself. "Never mind," I thought. "God knows." Going to my Christian neighbour's house, to collect my twin daughters who were playing at her house, I could hardly contain my excitement. 'You can borrow my computer,' she said as I explained what the Lord had shown me. I could not believe it, everything seemed to be falling into place. Now that I had the computer, I had to write the vision. The vision being what the book's aim was and its purpose was. It was how I, as a black female had overcome my battles with domestic violence, drugs, prejudice and spiritual forces in Christ and to testify that Jesus is the Christ and He is the God of all nations. My target audience was everyone ranging from age 15 years upwards. In writing my story, I would fulfil the vision of the book from what I could see. The cover I had seen spoke volumes to me (see cover of 'From Darkness to Light' by Fiona Lynch)

Questions:

1. What is your vision for your story?

2. What are you hoping to achieve?

3. Who is your target audience and why are they?

Take some time to think this through and write your answers down. You may already have the draft of your manuscript but thinking this through will help you filter out where you may have gone off track in respect of the vision and aim of what you are trying to achieve.

Your Title

Your title should be according to who your audience is and what you are writing about. For example, my book 'Created to be a Woman - Rediscover who you Are' is aimed at women who are seeking direction and/or have got to a place where they are stuck and need that push forward, whereas my book 'From Darkness to Light' - a true story is directed at all ages over the age of fifteen and is for anyone who enjoys a true story. The subheadings give an idea of what the main title is about. When writing and editing your manuscript keep your title in mind as it will remind you also of what you are trying to achieve and the journey that you are taking your reader on.

Questions:

1. What is the title of your manuscript?

2. Does your title speak about what you are producing?

Time Frames

I use this quote, 'time waits for no one.' The Clock is always ticking. Setting a time frame to prepare your document will give you something to aim for, a goal/target. Without time frames your idea or draft manuscript can end up gathering dust for years. Tell someone what you are doing and tell them when it will be done, you will then hold yourself accountable to achieve your goal. But I must stress nothing happens before the appointed time but getting prepared is important for that time.

It took seven years for my first book 'From Darkness to Light' to come into publication. Each year from the year I began to write my book, I kept telling everyone it would be out the following year. This was contrary to what the Lord was telling me. The lord kept saying, 'It will be launched at the same time as your ministry.' I had been called to set up and Pastor a Church and the vision of the Church was far away. So, at times I felt like ripping my book up and forgetting all about it. I even tried to find a publisher to publish it, but with no joy. Until, although frustrated, I surrendered 'From Darkness Light,' to the lord, trusting the word He had given me. He knows when we are ready and the timing for all that He has given to us. However, this does not mean that we should sit on what we have. It is important to step out. Finally, in October 2008, 'From Darkness to Light' was launched not long after the ministry the Lord had given me, which was launched in July 2008. The book with the same cover which I had seen in the vision in 2001, was now a reality. I did not pay for the book to be published. God showed me how to self-publish and the publishing company that I was to publish with, had the book cover on offer for free, which was also in the vision. The appointed time had now come, and my manuscript was ready for that time.

Questions:

1. When would you like your manuscript to be ready for publication? Put in a time frame. i.e. A time frame for drafting, editing and completion even if you are not sure of the date for publication. I have many other drafts which I am getting ready.

(a) Drafted by …………………

(b) Edited by …………………..

(c) Completed by or Published by …………………

Do not worry if you go slightly over your time frames, just give yourself an extension and keep on going.

Your Story Line

Your story line is what will keep your audience engaged. For example, in song writing it is the chorus that keeps the singer engaged in the song. The chorus is repetitive and is usually more melodious than the verses and takes the singer to a climax whereas the verses speak of what the song is about. Therefore, in every story, course etc there is a beginning, middle and end. The beginning is like the roadway to the middle of the story where there should be a form of climax, like the chorus and should keep the reader engaged to the end of the story/course.

Question:

1. What is your story line? Do a timeline of events for your fiction or non-fiction book. If it is a course, write out your course outline. i.e. if it is a nonfiction book – childhood – young adult – adult. Within these stages note down key events that are relevant to your story.

Making Your Manuscript Clear

Initially writing my story was easy. The Holy Spirit would wake me up even in the night to give me snippets of it. Everything would be brought back to remembrance bit by bit that I had gone through in the chapters of my life. I felt I had the permission to write what I wanted even if it was in anger for all the things that had been done to me. As I re-lived my life, I became more whole again. It took around six weeks for me to write out my first draft. I typed constantly, morning, noon and night. I just could not stop typing. Then the crunch came. After giving it to a couple of people to read, who said it was fine, I gave my book to a pastor friend of mine to read who had previously published a book. He took great care of my draft manuscript to the point of binding it for me. When he gave me his feedback, he told me the truth! I had to make my vision clear. I needed to stick to the aim and the purpose of the book. He told me I had too many characters. I needed to have main characters and have conversations between them in my story. I needed to decide what was relevant and what was not, and I needed to make it flow by keeping to the point. I am most grateful to him as later when I read back what I had written did not flow.

Action:

Decide what is necessary and what is not in your manuscript. Your audience is who you must think about when you are writing. Read back to yourself as though you are the reader and you will see what needs to be added and what needs to be taken out.

Characters

When writing non-fiction and fiction books, choose your characters carefully. Think about a favourite film or TV programme. They have the main characters and they also have some extras, but your main characters are the ones who will carry the story line to the end. For example, in a non-fiction and fiction book you will have a main character and the key people surrounding their lives that make the story. Too many characters can make the story boring and the reader will have to try and remember who everyone is if different characters pop up all the time. In my book 'From Darkness to Light' I am the main character and the people who have had the most impact in my life whether good or bad are the main characters that make my story; however, the story is about me and my journey.

Question:

Who are your main characters? Describe them and their part in the story line. This will help you when putting your story together.

Description

For any genre, description is important. Describing characters and scenery for stories will enable the reader to visualise and feel what they are reading. It will give them insight into your story and will speak to them. In respect of teaching books/courses and magazines there should be a correlation between each session that relates to the name of the course or magazine. For example, my teaching course, 'The basics of Discipleship' – laying the foundation, is about teaching a new Christian about pre-salvation, salvation and post salvation in the hope that they will have foundational knowledge in Christ to build on for their next stage of their Christian walk. Therefore, it was important for me to describe the meaning of some of the scriptures so that they can study for themselves.

Teaching Books/Courses & Magazines

In respect of the above, the content is usually factual, therefore whatever you teach would require evidence for what you are teaching. They can be based on life experiences, scriptures, statistics or even research. So, it is important to know your subject. If someone asks you what your course or magazine is about, you should be able to answer them by giving a short summary about it. This is also the case for any work that you produce.

Question:

1. What is your course/magazine about? Write a summary of what you would say if you were asked about it.

Editing

Now that you have drafted your project, it will need editing. I had edited my first book 'From Darkness to Light' ten times before I made the decision to take the plunge and publish it and I would say it will always be a work in progress. Many authors have several editions for their books, because as time goes on, they have more to add or even take away from their work. Therefore, we can have for example a first edition, a second edition and a third edition.

In editing my book, I first took out all the irrelevant details and characters and added a bit more creativity to make my story interesting as advised. I wanted the reader to hear my voice as I took them through my journey of how I went into darkness and how I entered the light.

After the ninth attempt of going through my book, an ex-Sunday school teacher went through my manuscript for the last time. I was fortunate enough to have met him one day whilst out shopping and he was more than happy to help me. Although it was not as polished as I wanted it to be, I made the decision, on the advice of friends, to publish it.

There are four elements to consider when editing your project:

1. Correcting - Mistakes and grammar.

2. Condensing - Taking out irrelevant information and shortening paragraphs.

3. Modifying - Making slight changes and/or rearranging paragraphs and chapters to ensure consistency.

4. Flowing between paragraphs - Ensuring that the paragraphs are continuing from one to another.

Readers Reviews

It is good to get reader's reviews once your manuscript is prepared. This could be given by someone you know such as a family member or a very good friend. Although I did have a couple of good friends who read my first book, they did not see the flaws and could only see all good in it. I had known that my manuscript needed brushing up just one more time, but they loved the story which was what I wanted reviewing. But be careful who you give your work to as they may lose it or even copy it although your work is copyrighted once you have penned it on paper. We will look at copyrighting in the next session.

Question:

Do you have someone that could read your book and give you an honest review? Write down the things that you know need to be analysed before handing it over for someone to read. They may not even agree with all your work however, you will need to be definite about what you want.

Conclusion

Now that your manuscript is prepared, it is now time to take it through the publishing process.

To summarise, there are three key points in writing your book. 1. Your vision, 2. Your aim and 3. Your audience and why are they your audience. These points can be applied to any writing project. In everything there is a beginning, middle and end. Put a time limit on your project so that you will complete it. In writing my first book, I went through a lot of frustrations trying to make my story plain for the reader. I had to make it readable to all cultures so that anyone could pick it up and read it. In doing so when editing my manuscript, the reader was on my mind. There were times that I wanted to just rip it up and throw it away and times when I really did not believe I would see it published. If you follow the tips in this session you will have the foundation to take your work to the next step.

From Manuscript to Publication

Publication is 'the preparation and issuing of a book, journal or piece of music for sale.' (online dictionary)

Preparing your manuscript for publication can be a long drawn out process. I know this as aforesaid it took seven years before my first book was published and it is still a work in progress. Therefore, some books have different editions because they have either added or extracted things from their books. With regard to producing regular magazine publications and regular booklets there will also be ongoing editions but once you have your format and style it will be easy to extract and add what materials you would like.

Once published, note that not everyone will like your work! There will be those who will find something to say and those who will just be happy. My first book had a rise in sales at one point due to negative critics.

Decision:

Are you and your manuscript ready for publication?

Yes/No – If no, what do you need to do?

Publishing Your Manuscript

There are four ways that you can produce your manuscript for publication.

1. Hard Copy – A book, course, magazine that is in paper form.

2. eBook – Available through kindle, iTunes, Google play and many other applications.

3. Audio – This speaks for itself and there are many programs that you can use to do this.

4. Online – This is especially for online magazine's and courses which can be produced through online teaching programmes.

Question:

1. What form would you like your manuscript to be published in? Write a list then choose one form to start with and then progress from there.

Publishing Avenues

There are three avenues in which a manuscript can be published:

1. Traditional publishing through established publishing companies and you would most certainly need to go through an agent.

2. Self-publishing through different publishing companies of which there are many.

3. Through a printing company where you can bulk print your books.

Traditional Publishing

Traditional publishing is now becoming less common and many are now turning to self-publishing. When sending your manuscript to a traditional publisher, it is important to prepare yourself for rejection. Not every publisher will see your vision for your manuscript or even appreciate the hard work and effort that you have put into your manuscript. I tried three publishers (not many) and all three rejected my work. They did not see the vision for what I had, or they were not accepting this type of story.

As a Christian I knew that God had given me the vision and had inspired me to write my book and would somehow direct me to have it in print. So, I waited patiently...

With perseverance, patience and faith in what you have, you will succeed.

For those of you who are led to seek a traditional publisher you will need to do three things:

1. Provide a covering letter including why they should be interested in your book, what makes your book different, who is your audience and what have you done to market your book.

2. A synopsis. This is an overview of what your book is about.

3. Three chapters from your manuscript in one and a half line spacing.

Although the above is what is usually required some publishers may have different requirements. However, they all usually involve having the rights over your book.

Out of the three traditional publishers that rejected my work, I did get a response from one of them who wanted to read all my manuscript. It was rejected because I was not in agreement with what they wanted me to do. A lady was assigned by them as a reader of manuscripts and would criticise accordingly. Although some of her criticism was constructive i.e. too many characters, she brought her own feelings into it. She did not believe I suffered from racism and became defensive, also she found the darkness of my life overwhelming. She even said she had never read a book like it and that nowhere had she read a testimony where someone had been through some of the things I had and that she believed there was a market for my book.

But... it was still rejected. The editor wanted me to rewrite it as though it was a fiction story. This was not what God wanted and it was not the vision for the book, so I walked away.

It is important to stick to your plan and to not be swayed due to desperation. Place value on your vision.

Feeling disappointed, I went through my book one more time, taking out the characters that were not relevant and laid my book down to rest until one day I remembered someone had mentioned something about self-publishing and the Lord began to convict me about doing this. I felt that God did not want me to sell the rights of my story to another person and did not want me to change what He had done through me.

Scanning the internet for self-publishing companies, I first came across one that stood out to me and requested a brochure. When the brochure arrived, and I saw the prices I knew at that time I could never afford it. Later I continued my search and typed in free publishing services in the Google search bar. I believed since God had given the vision, He would give the provision. This was when I stumbled across Lulu.com. A free self-publishing service which appeared too good to be true. I registered with part fear that I may be giving my details to a scam website as nothing is usually free in this world without a catch! I did some research and spoke with one of their recommended editors via email and sent her a sample of three chapters. She recommended that Lulu was very good and that there was no catch. She also said that my story was very good. Although she was not a Christian, she was intrigued and wanted to read more. She advised that I did not need a professional editor and that if I knew an English teacher, I should ask them to look at it and correct my grammar. Having a professional editor say this gave me great inspiration. Besides I was anxious for someone to be honest in the right way. I knew my book needed to be polished.

A preacher once said, you can do anything if you gather your information and apply it, so that was what I did. I read up on everything on self-publishing, about prices, royalties, formatting, book covers, ISBN numbers and marketing. I gained all the knowledge that I needed to get myself going. It was around this time that I met Bill aforesaid, my previous Sunday school teacher who eventually edited my book with me. Once we had edited the final copy, I began to format it according to the information I found.

Question:

1. Are you prepared to put in the work that self-publishing requires? Or would you prefer to seek a traditional publisher?

Self-Publishing

To self-publish takes a lot of time and effort, but with a bit of determination you will get there in the end. And after doing it once, it will be easier to do it again. I chose Lulu.com as it has a lot of information to enable you to have a completed piece of work prepared in the right format for your book and they only sells books. Of course, there are others like Create Space through Amazon. However, with most self-publishing companies there is a price to pay if you cannot do the work yourself as you will have to pay for their services such as editing, designing and formatting amongst many others. If you can do it yourself, it is all free to publish. The only costs that you pay in these self-publishing companies is for the cost of your book when you buy it in hard copy, but this is the wholesale price and not the retail price. In respect of eBooks they are free to download if you require a copy.

Templates

Your book will need to have the right template for printing. Margins will need to be adjusted to give room for printing. You can download a template from Lulu.com for your manuscript. For my book 'From Darkness to Light' I used the US standard trade which is 6 x 9in. It was recommended at the time as it could be distributed almost anywhere. I now use A5 as it is a good size that can slip into a bag without taking up too much room.

I noted that when you download a word template you can also download a template for your book cover, making it easier for those who would like to design their own cover. When choosing a template, be mindful of the book size if you are trying to get your book into a shop. Shops have limited shelf space therefore if your book is a big size you may have less opportunities to have your book put on their shelf.

Action:

Choose a size template for your manuscript and then copy and paste your manuscript onto it. You will now have it in the format to work on for the next stage.

Formatting Your Manuscript

There are many ways to make your manuscript presentable and this can be dependent upon what you are writing. I have listed a few.

1. **The Heading** – This can be produced in bold, capitals and underlined etc and you could use a different font from the rest of the book, but it really is down to each individual and on what you are writing.

2. **The Spacing** – Spacing is also dependable on what you are writing. For example, in my book 'From Darkness to Light' I have used one and a half line spacing. This was not actually deliberate but when it arrived, and many had read it and commented on the spacing saying how it made it easy to read I was happy with this. This book can be read by many, especially if someone has difficulty in reading or have problems with their sight.

3. **Drop Caps** - Drop caps is when the first letter on the page of every new chapter is in a larger font. This font can be in a different font from the fonts used in the overall text. This gives your book some character and style. I would recommend this style for story books. Also, with story books it is recommended to start each chapter a third of the way down the page, again giving character and style to your book.

4. **Fonts** – Bold, Italics, Underline – I would recommend that your font size is 11, using Verdana. If you are using Arial, you may have to make it larger as it reads smaller. But each writer will have their own preferences. However, when writing magazines and newsletters etc it will have to be a case of trying different styles to see what looks best for the style of your magazine and for your audience.

6. **Photographs and Pictures** – Many people use photographs when writing autobiographies, but it is a personal choice. Pictures are usually used in children's books

5. **Page Numbering** – If you are not using centred page numbers then your page numberings will have to be done on the opposite side of each page so that when you turn the page it is in the right place (please see books that have page numbers that are not centred for reference).

Presentation

To polish up your book, presentation at the beginning and ending of your work is important. Many people read the inside pages first and the back page to get an idea of what your book is about before they decide to read it.

1. **Foreword** – This is written by someone else who knows you and can endorse you and your work.

2. **Dedication** – This is who you would like to acknowledge for their support and encouragement during your time in writing your book

3. **Introduction/Preface** – This is what your book is about.

4. **Contents Page** – This is a list of your chapters and page numbers so that the reader can look up whichever chapter they would like to read and to reference back to.

5. **Epilogue** – This is where you give an overview of where you are at now.

Action:

Note down the list of things that you need to do and work on your presentation.

Quoting From Others and Scriptures

If you are quoting other writers work, they should be written as they are written down from the writer stating the writers name. If you are quoting from the bible it must be written in the exact format from the version that you are reciting from, i.e. put commas, italics etc where necessary and always state what version the scriptures are from on the copyright page.

Copyright Page

The copyright page is the page which sets out the legal rights and protects your work although your work is protected once it is an original piece of work. There is a lot of information on the internet about copyrighting your work.

Example Copyright:

Your Book Cover

Once you have formatted and uploaded your work the next step is to add your book cover. On Lulu.com you have the option to either choose a book cover from their cover gallery or upload your own. I was amazed how easy it was. The cover that I chose was one that was in the vision when God first showed me, I was going to write my book, From Darkness to Light. So, I happily uploaded it adding to it what I wanted with Bill writing the blurb on the back. The blurb being a short description of your book to promote your material. Sometimes people will have reviews of what others have said on the back of their book as many readers will read this before deciding whether to buy your book.

Please note there are many programmes that you can use to create your own book cover.

Question:

1. Have you decided what your book cover will look like? Write a description of it.

ISBN Number

The next step will be to purchase an ISBN number which is free through Lulu.com whilst using them in distribution. I discovered this made no difference as to who the publisher is because on Lulu.com you keep all copyrights and you are in fact still the publisher as you are self-publishing.

An ISBN number is the International Standard Book Number. This number is assigned to your publication so that book can be identified internationally as your book. Without an ISBN number you will not be able to have your book in the distribution channels because it would be impossible to trace the publication back to you as the author for you to be paid royalties on any sales. However, you can choose to distribute your publication through a personal website and through different organisations by selling them copies of your book at discount price.

Your ISBN should be put on the copyright page (as shown before) and on the back of your book cover.

Example - ISBN 978-1-4092-1218-8 (From Darkness to Light)

An ISBN number can be purchased from your local ISBN agency or through a publishing company. Because I had published my book with Lulu.com, I was allocated a free ISBN which they automatically printed on the back cover of my book with a barcode. The ISBN was assigned to my project immediately once I had started the publication process. This makes publication easier as you can add it to your manuscript before uploading your file.

Pricing Your Book and Royalties

Now that you have done all the hard work, you will now want to be paid! Every publisher will have a price that they set for your book so that they can be paid, you can be paid, and the retailer can be paid. For example, my book 'From Darkness to Light' is sold for £11.98 through Lulu.com and Amazon and many other retail outlets although some have reduced their prices. When someone makes an order through Amazon, Amazon gets a percentage, I get a percentage and Lulu.com receive a percentage. When my book is purchased directly through Lulu.com the royalties are higher as there is no middle man such as Amazon. However, when I buy my book myself, I pay a wholesale price as Lulu.com needs to charge for the printing costs plus their own revenue but it is a lot cheaper than the retail price (as is the case for any self-publishing companies). I can therefore sell my book personally for less at £10.00 should I wish to.

Action:

Once all the above is done you can now order your book to proof read it!

Proof Reading

Now that you have published your work, it must be approved. With self-publishing it is recommended that you order a copy before approving it because once you have approved your book, it can now be distributed through Amazon and many other online book stores. Therefore, it is important to read through your finished production carefully. The day my first book arrived I was elated. But whilst reading through it, the mistakes were more noticeable.

After re-editing my book, again, I ordered another copy and again I was not happy with it so had one more go at editing it and reading through it once again in book format, before surrendering to the fact that my book was not ever going to be perfect. After all, it was my first book and my first edition. So, after one more go at editing it with Bill, I approved my book and officially published it!

In Print

Seeing my book on Amazon (and their international sites), Barnes and Noble and other online book stores appeared surreal. I had achieved my goal. After seven years of writing, editing and formatting my book, it was now in print and available to buy.

From Publication to Marketing

Now that your book is in print it is now time to get some book sales. Your sales should not be focused on how much money you want to make but on what your book is trying to achieve and to get some media coverage. By focusing on the aim of the book you will market it to the right audience.

The following are some book marketing ideas that you can utilise whether you have published with a traditional publisher or self-publisher (unless the traditional publisher has bought your copyrights then they will do everything for you).

Book Launches

It is good to do a book launch in your local community to give recognition of the work you have done. People who know you will spread the word about what you have achieved and will recommend your book to their friends and family.

Below is a list of places where you could launch your book (and of course do book signings):

1. At your local library

2. Local community centres

3. Local Hotels

4. Local organisations such as Churches and groups relevant to what your book is about.

5. Local Supermarkets such as Tesco's.

All the above welcome local authors.

Action:

Book a date, time and venue for your book launch. Take a leap of faith and believe in what you have… Write down the places that you have contacted and where you have booked your book launch and book signings.

Advertising

Once you have booked your book launch slots, you must now advertise your events. The following are suggestions of where you could advertise:

- Your local radio station by asking them to speak to their audience about your book or ask if you can attend at the station and talk about your publication through an interview.

- Your local bookshop - I was fortunate enough to have my book in a local bookshop through networking at a Christian Writers Group in which I became one of their speakers on a few occasions. Bookshops are reluctant to take on books as they only have limited shelving space although they can order your books if a customer requests it.

- Your local Newspaper – they welcome stories

- Your local community Centres

- Word of Mouth

Your Flyer and Promotion Materials

To advertise your launch, you will need to produce a flyer to put around for example your local shops and library and as many places as possible. The heading could say something like 'local resident publishes his/her book' then put the title of your book, your name and details of where and when. Try and make your flyer catchy and inviting and always put details of where they can purchase your book and your contact details should you wish to be contacted.

At your event you could have some promotion materials such as pens, order forms, vouchers and do a raffle of your book and of course sign your books with your contact details in. Business cards are always good to have handy wherever you go and always have books with you ready to sell.

- Be bold and confident about what you have achieved and be prepared for criticism. Criticism resulted in my book sales going up!! It brought about curiosity as to what my book is about...

Question:

Are you ready to promote your publication? – Time waits for no one; it is your purpose and destiny that matters.

Social Media

Modern technology is moving fast, and I have listed below several social media sites where you can market your work.

1. Facebook – Have a Facebook Page about your publication. Talk about it and put excerpts up and discuss them.

2. Instagram – Have an Instagram page and talk about your publications.

3. Twitter – Do regular tweets.

4. Blog – Start blogging on your subject before your book is released and continue thereafter.

5. Email Signature – Put your details at the end of your emails with a link to where your book can be purchased.

6. Websites – see my websites for examples:

   www.lulu.com/fionalynch

7. Videos and book trailers.

8. Local talks on subjects to do with your book.

9. Get as many people to write reviews about your book.

10. Have your books with you wherever you go so that you are prepared to sell them.

There are also several other places that you can market yourself and your work such as Hubpages, Authors Den, Google Circle and through email marketing (sending emails to your email contacts). There are so many ways through social media that you can market your book. Explore!

Note:

Congratulations on going through this guide. You now have the basic knowledge to start your journey in writing, publishing and marketing your book.

Value your work. I have made the mistake of having an expensive hobby (as my mentor once said) by giving away books rather than selling them because I have wanted others to read them. If they really want to read your book, they will buy it!

www.ingramcontent.com/pod-product-compliance
Lightning Source LLC
Chambersburg PA
CBHW061231180526
45170CB00003B/1245